EMBRACING DIVERSITY:

AFRICAN MIGRANTS IMPACT ON Global Communities

WILLIAM I. JOHNSON

All rights reserved. No part of this publication may be reproduced, distributed, or transmitted in any form or by any means, including photocopying, recording, or other electronic or mechanical methods, without the prior written permission of the publisher, except in the case of brief quotations embodied in critical reviews and certain other noncommercial uses permitted by copyright law.

Copyright ©William I. Johnson, 2023

Table of contents

Introduction

In a world that is becoming increasingly interconnected, migration has emerged as a defining feature of our times. Within this dynamic landscape, African migrants have played a significant role in shaping the global community. They bring with them unique perspectives, rich cultural traditions, and a wealth of experiences that enrich the tapestry of societies they join.

"Embracing Diversity: African Migrants' Impact on Global Communities" is a captivating exploration of the journeys, contributions, and challenges faced by African migrants across the globe. It delves into the stories of individuals who have left their homelands in search of better opportunities, and the profound impact they have had on the communities they now call home.

Through the pages of this book, readers will embark on a remarkable journey, discovering the resilience, determination, and courage that characterizes the African migrant experience. From the bustling streets of metropolises to the quiet corners of rural towns, this collection of narratives paints a vivid picture of the multifaceted contributions that African migrants make in diverse fields such as arts, culture, business, academia, and humanitarian work.

Moreover, "Embracing Diversity" explores the transformative power of intercultural exchange, highlighting how African migrants have fostered understanding, challenged stereotypes, and promoted social cohesion within their host communities. It sheds light on the positive impact they have on local economies, innovation, and social development, offering fresh perspectives on the dynamics of globalization.

This book not only celebrates the achievements of African migrants but also addresses the complex issues they face, such as integration, discrimination, and identity. It serves as a platform for dialogue, inviting readers to reflect on the importance of inclusivity, respect for diversity, and the collective responsibility to build welcoming societies.

"Embracing Diversity: African Migrants' Impact on Global Communities" is a compelling testament to the power of human migration and the immeasurable value that African migrants bring to the world. It invites readers to embrace diversity, challenge preconceptions, and recognize the immense potential that lies within the rich tapestry of global communities.

Chapter 1

ROOT CAUSES OF MIGRATION

It is important to examine the underlying reasons why Africans choose to migrate to Europe. Factors such as poverty, conflict, political instability, and environmental degradation can all contribute to displacement and migration.

The root causes of African migration are complex and multifaceted, with a combination of push and pull factors influencing people's decisions to leave their home countries.

Key Factors Contributing To African Migration

ECONOMIC FACTORS

Economic instability, poverty, and lack of job opportunities are major drivers of migration. Many African countries face high unemployment rates, particularly among the youth, and limited prospects for economic advancement. People often migrate in search of better economic opportunities and the hope for a higher standard of living. Economic factors play a significant role in driving African migration.

Several Key Factors Contribute To This Phenomenon

- **Limited Job Opportunities:** High unemployment rates, particularly among young people, are prevalent in many African countries. Limited job opportunities and a lack of formal employment prospects push individuals to seek better economic conditions elsewhere. They may migrate to countries with stronger economies that offer more employment opportunities and higher wages.

- **Poverty and Inequality:** Widespread poverty and economic inequality are pervasive issues in Africa. Many individuals and families struggle to meet their basic needs and have limited access to essential services such as education and healthcare. Economic migration offers the potential for improved living standards and the ability to support their families by sending remittances back home.

- **Informal Economy:** The informal economy, including street vending, small-scale agriculture, and informal labor, is a significant source of employment for many Africans. However, this sector often lacks stability, security, and formal protections. As a result, individuals may migrate to countries with more developed and formalized economies to seek better working conditions and opportunities in the formal sector.

- **Urbanization and Rural-Urban Disparities:** Rapid urbanization in African countries has led to significant disparities between rural and urban areas. Many rural communities face limited economic prospects, inadequate infrastructure, and a lack of basic services. People from these regions may migrate to cities or other countries in search of better economic opportunities and improved living conditions.

- **Global Economic Disparities:** The global economic disparities between Africa and more developed regions contribute to migration. Individuals may seek to access economic opportunities, higher wages, and better living standards offered by countries in Europe, North America, or other regions with stronger economies.

- **Brain Drain:** Africa also experiences the phenomenon of "brain drain," where highly skilled professionals, such as doctors, engineers, and academics, leave their home countries to seek better employment opportunities abroad. This loss of skilled workers can further hinder economic development in their home countries.

It is important to note that economic migration is a complex issue influenced by a combination of factors. Addressing economic factors contributing to African migration requires efforts to promote economic development, reduce poverty and inequality, create job opportunities, and improve the overall socio-economic conditions within African countries. International cooperation, investment, and fair trade policies that support inclusive growth and sustainable development can help address these economic drivers of migration.

POLITICAL INSTABILITY AND CONFLICT

Ongoing political instability, armed conflicts, and human rights abuses in certain African countries force people to flee their homes. These conflicts often result from ethnic tensions, political repression, and competition for resources. The desire for safety and security drives individuals to seek refuge in other countries, both within Africa and beyond.

Political instability and conflict have long been significant factors contributing to African migration. The complex interplay of these issues has driven large-scale migration within the continent and across its borders.

Several Key Factors Contribute To This Situation:

1. **Civil Wars and Armed Conflicts:** Africa has witnessed numerous civil wars and armed conflicts, often fueled by ethnic, religious, or political divisions. These conflicts create widespread violence, displacement, and human rights abuses, leading to large-scale migration. People flee their homes in search of safety and refuge, often crossing borders to neighboring countries or embarking on perilous journeys to other regions.

2. **Governance Challenges:** Weak governance, corruption, and lack of political stability undermine socio-economic development in many African countries. These conditions can lead to social unrest, economic disparities, and a lack of opportunities, which in turn prompt people to migrate in search of better prospects and stability elsewhere.

3. **Political Repression:** Repressive regimes, authoritarian rule, and human rights violations are

prevalent in some African nations. These conditions can lead to persecution, political oppression, and restrictions on personal freedoms, prompting individuals to seek asylum or migrate to countries with more democratic systems and respect for human rights.

4. **Economic Factors:** Economic instability, poverty, and lack of job opportunities contribute significantly to African migration. High unemployment rates, inadequate infrastructure, and limited access to education and healthcare push people to seek better economic prospects in other countries, particularly in regions with more robust economies.

5. **Environmental Challenges:** Environmental factors, such as droughts, desertification, and climate change, have a significant impact on migration patterns. These issues can lead to resource scarcity, food insecurity, and displacement, compelling people to leave their homes in search of more habitable regions.

6. **Regional Spillover Effects:** Conflict and instability in one African country often have regional spillover effects, exacerbating tensions and creating a ripple effect of migration. Neighboring

countries may experience increased migration flows as they become destinations or transit points for those seeking safety or opportunities.

Addressing these root causes requires a comprehensive approach, including efforts to promote peace and security, strengthen governance and institutions, foster economic development, tackle climate change, and uphold human rights. International cooperation, humanitarian assistance, and sustainable development initiatives can play a crucial role in alleviating the pressures that drive African migration.

ENVIRONMENTAL FACTORS

Environmental challenges such as droughts, desertification, deforestation, and natural disasters contribute to migration. Climate change has exacerbated these issues, leading to food insecurity and the displacement of communities dependent on agriculture and natural resources. People may migrate in search of more favorable environmental conditions or to escape the consequences of environmental degradation.

Environmental Factors Significantly Contribute To African Migration, As Individuals And Communities

Are Often Compelled To Leave Their Homes Due To The Following Reasons:

1. **Climate Change and Natural Disasters:** Africa is particularly vulnerable to the impacts of climate change, including increased droughts, desertification, floods, and storms. These environmental changes can lead to crop failures, livestock losses, and the destruction of homes and infrastructure, forcing people to migrate in search of more habitable and secure areas.

2. **Resource Scarcity and Land Degradation:** Environmental degradation, such as deforestation, soil erosion, and depletion of natural resources, poses significant challenges in many African regions. As land becomes less fertile and resources diminish, communities dependent on agriculture and natural Resource-based livelihoods may experience economic hardship, food insecurity, and displacement, prompting migration to more sustainable environments.

3. **Water Scarcity:** Water scarcity is a pressing environmental concern in many parts of Africa. Dwindling water supplies, especially in arid and semi-arid regions, can disrupt agriculture, affect

livestock herding, and lead to inadequate access to clean drinking water. These challenges drive migration as people search for areas with better water resources to sustain their livelihoods and meet their basic needs.

4. **Desertification and Land Encroachment:** Desertification, the process by which fertile land transforms into desert, is a significant issue in parts of Africa. It can result from factors such as deforestation, overgrazing, and unsustainable land management practices. As desertification expands, agricultural productivity declines, and communities are forced to abandon their land, contributing to migration patterns.

5. **Coastal Erosion and Rising Sea Levels:** African countries with extensive coastlines, such as those in West Africa, are particularly vulnerable to coastal erosion and rising sea levels. These environmental changes can lead to the loss of homes, displacement of communities, and salinization of agricultural land, driving migration away from affected coastal areas.

6. **Conflict over Natural Resources:** Environmental factors can also contribute to conflicts and resource-related disputes. Competition for scarce

resources, such as fertile land, water sources, and mineral deposits, can escalate tensions and lead to armed conflicts. Environmental degradation and resource-driven conflicts often contribute to displacement and migration as people seek safety and stability.

Addressing environmental factors contributing to African migration requires efforts to mitigate and adapt to the impacts of climate change, promote sustainable land and resource management practices, and build resilience in vulnerable communities. International cooperation, investment in renewable energy, conservation efforts, and the implementation of climate change adaptation strategies are crucial for minimizing the environmental drivers of migration and supporting sustainable development in Africa.

DEMOGRAPHIC PRESSURES

Rapid population growth in many African countries strains available resources and infrastructure. The lack of access to education, healthcare, and other essential services, combined with the inability of governments to adequately address these challenges, can drive people to migrate in search of better living conditions for themselves and their families.

Demographic pressures are significant contributors to African migration, as population dynamics and related factors can drive people to seek opportunities and improved living conditions elsewhere.

Some Of The Key Demographic Factors Contributing To African Migration Are:

1. **Population Growth:** Africa has one of the highest population growth rates in the world. The rapid increase in population, coupled with limited resources and economic opportunities, can put pressure on communities and contribute to migration. The need to find alternative livelihoods and access basic services can drive individuals and families to migrate in search of better prospects.

2. **Youth Bulge:** Africa has a significant youth bulge, with a large proportion of its population being young people. The lack of sufficient educational and employment opportunities for this growing youth population can create economic challenges and social tensions, prompting migration as young

individuals seek better prospects and a brighter future elsewhere.

3. **Urbanization:** Rapid urbanization is occurring across Africa, with people migrating from rural areas to cities in search of economic opportunities and improved living conditions. The concentration of population in urban areas can put a strain on infrastructure, housing, and services, leading to socio-economic challenges and pushing individuals to migrate further, including internationally, in search of better prospects.

4. **Gender Dynamics:** Gender dynamics also play a role in African migration. In some cases, men may migrate first, leaving behind their families, in search of employment opportunities. This can be driven by economic factors, societal expectations, and the desire to support their families. In turn, women may follow later to reunite with their male family members or to seek better opportunities themselves, contributing to migration patterns.

5. **Lack of Education and Skills Development:** Limited access to quality education and skills development programs can hinder economic opportunities and social mobility. Individuals, particularly young people, may migrate to countries

or regions that offer better educational and training opportunities to enhance their skills and increase their employability.

6. **Family Reunification:** Family reunification is a common driver of migration, where individuals migrate to join family members who have already settled in another country or region. This can be motivated by the desire for improved economic prospects, access to education, or to escape adverse living conditions in their home countries.

Addressing demographic pressures contributing to African migration requires a multi-faceted approach. It involves investing in education and skills development, creating job opportunities, promoting inclusive economic growth, and implementing policies that address the needs and aspirations of the growing youth population. Additionally, targeted efforts to improve living conditions, access to basic services, and social support systems in both rural and urban areas can help alleviate the demographic pressures that drive migration.

LACK OF DEVELOPMENT AND INFRASTRUCTURE

Insufficient investment in social and economic development, including infrastructure, healthcare, education, and governance, hampers opportunities within African countries. Limited access to basic services and a perceived lack of prospects can motivate individuals to seek better living conditions elsewhere.

The lack of development and infrastructure in Africa significantly contributes to migration. Insufficient development and inadequate infrastructure can create economic, social, and environmental challenges that drive individuals and communities to migrate.

Here Are Some Key Ways In Which The Lack Of Development And Infrastructure Contributes To African Migration:

1. **Limited Economic** Opportunities: Inadequate development hampers economic growth and job creation, resulting in limited economic opportunities for individuals and communities. This lack of employment prospects, particularly in

rural areas, pushes people to migrate in search of better livelihoods and income-generating activities elsewhere.

2. **Poor Basic Services:** Insufficient infrastructure leads to inadequate access to basic services such as education, healthcare, clean water, and sanitation. Communities lacking access to these essential services face higher levels of poverty, poor health conditions, and limited educational opportunities. This can prompt individuals and families to migrate to areas with better infrastructure and access to services.

3. **Food Insecurity:** Agricultural development is crucial for food security and rural development. However, inadequate infrastructure, limited access to markets, and poor farming techniques can hinder agricultural productivity and contribute to food insecurity. When communities face persistent food shortages and struggle to meet their nutritional needs, migration becomes a means to access food and improve their overall well-being.

4. **Inadequate Transportation and Connectivity:** Weak transportation networks, including roads, railways, and ports, restrict the movement of people and goods. This lack of connectivity limits trade

hampers economic development and isolates communities from essential services. Migration can be driven by the desire to access better transportation networks and more connected regions that offer improved opportunities for trade and economic growth.

5. **Environmental Challenges:** The lack of infrastructure and development exacerbates the impacts of environmental challenges, such as droughts, floods, and land degradation. Without proper infrastructure, communities struggle to cope with and adapt to these environmental pressures, leading to increased vulnerability and a higher likelihood of migration in search of more sustainable and resilient environments.

6. **Urban-Rural Disparities:** Disparities between urban and rural areas are often pronounced in terms of development and infrastructure. Cities tend to have better infrastructure, services, and employment opportunities, which attract individuals from rural areas. The lack of balanced development between urban and rural regions can drive migration as people seek better access to resources, services, and economic prospects in urban centers.

Addressing the lack of development and infrastructure requires targeted investments in key sectors such as education, healthcare, agriculture, transportation, and energy. It also involves promoting inclusive economic growth, enhancing connectivity, and improving access to basic services. Sustainable development initiatives, capacity building, and international cooperation can play a crucial role in alleviating the pressures that lead to African migration due to a lack of development and infrastructure.

GLOBAL INEQUALITIES AND THE PULL OF DEVELOPED COUNTRIES

Disparities in wealth, opportunities, and living standards between African countries and more developed nations create a pull factor for migration. The allure of better education, healthcare, employment opportunities, and social welfare systems in wealthier countries can incentivize individuals to migrate in search of a better future.

Global inequalities and the pull of developed countries are significant factors contributing to African migration. These dynamics create imbalances in economic opportunities, living standards, and access to resources, prompting individuals and communities to seek better prospects in more developed nations.

Here's How Global Inequalities And The Pull Of Developed Countries Contribute To African Migration:

1. **Economic Disparities:** Global economic inequalities create stark differences in income levels and job opportunities between developed and developing countries. African countries often face limited economic prospects, high poverty rates, and inadequate wages, prompting individuals to seek employment and higher incomes in developed countries with stronger economies.

2. **Higher Living Standards:** Developed countries typically offer higher living standards, including better access to education, healthcare, infrastructure, and social welfare systems. The availability of these improved services and overall quality of life acts as a pull factor for individuals and families who aspire to provide a better future for themselves and their children.

3. **Access to Education and Skills Development:** Developed countries often provide better

educational and skills development opportunities. Individuals may migrate to access quality education and training programs, especially in fields where there are labor shortages or greater demand in developed nations. This enables them to enhance their employability and seek higher-paying jobs.

4. **Political Stability and Security:** Political stability and security are attractive factors in developed countries. African nations experiencing political instability, conflict, and human rights abuses may drive individuals to migrate in search of safety, stability, and the protection of their fundamental rights and freedoms.

5. **Family Reunification and Social Networks:** The presence of family members, friends, or existing social networks in developed countries can serve as a pull factor for migration. The desire to reunite with loved ones or to benefit from established social support systems motivates individuals to migrate to countries where their connections are already settled.

6. **Migration Policies and Labor Demands:** Migration policies and labor demands in developed countries can influence migration patterns. When these countries have labor shortages or specific skill

requirements, they may implement immigration policies that attract workers from African countries to meet their workforce needs. Temporary work programs and the demand for specific skills can act as a pull factor for African migrants.

Addressing the pull of developed countries and global inequalities requires a comprehensive approach. It involves promoting inclusive and sustainable economic development within African nations, reducing poverty and inequality, enhancing education and skills development, strengthening governance, and improving access to basic services. Additionally, addressing global inequalities and creating fair and just migration policies can contribute to a more balanced and equitable migration system. International cooperation, dialogue, and collaboration are essential to addressing these complex challenges and ensuring that migration benefits both sending and receiving countries.

It is important to note that the causes of migration are interconnected, and multiple factors often contribute to an individual's decision to migrate. Addressing these root causes requires comprehensive and coordinated efforts, including investment in economic development, conflict resolution, environmental sustainability, and governance reforms, both within African countries and through international cooperation.

CHAPTER 2

IMMIGRATION POLICIES

Immigration policies for African migrants vary among countries and regions, and they can differ significantly based on the specific immigration laws, priorities, and circumstances of each destination country. While it is challenging to provide an exhaustive overview of immigration policies for African migrants in all countries.

Here Are Some Common Aspects And Considerations:

VISA REQUIREMENTS

African migrants often need to obtain visas to enter and stay legally in their destination country. The visa requirements may vary based on the purpose of travel, such as tourism, study, work, or family reunification. Different types of visas, such as short-term visitor visas, student visas, work permits, or family-sponsored visas, may be available.

Visa requirements for African migrants vary depending on the country they plan to visit or migrate to. The specific visa regulations and categories can differ significantly between countries, so it's important for African migrants to research and understand the visa requirements of their intended destination.

Here Are Some Common Visa Categories And Considerations:

1. Tourist/Visitor Visas: African migrants traveling for tourism or short-term visits typically need to obtain a tourist or visitor visa. These visas allow individuals to stay in the destination country for a limited period, usually for tourism, leisure, or visiting friends and family. The duration of stay and visa validity can vary depending on the country.

2. Student Visas: African students planning to pursue education in another country will generally require a student visa. These visas are issued to individuals accepted by an educational institution and allow them to reside in the destination country for the duration of their studies. Specific documentation, such as proof of enrollment and financial resources, may be required.

3. Work Permits/Employment Visas: African migrants seeking employment opportunities in another country usually need to obtain a work permit or employment visa. These visas allow individuals to work legally and often require sponsorship from an employer. Work permits may have specific requirements related to skill levels, labor market needs, and qualifications.

4. Business Visas: African migrants traveling for business purposes, such as attending conferences, meetings, or exploring business opportunities, may require a business visa. These visas typically have limitations on the types of activities allowed and the duration of stay. Documentation, such as invitation letters or proof of business engagement, may be required.

5. Family Reunification Visas: African migrants who have family members residing in another country may be eligible for family reunification visas. These visas allow them to join their immediate family members, such as spouses, parents, or children, who are already living in the destination country. Proof of the family relationship and financial support may be required.

6. Transit Visas: If African migrants are transiting through a country on their way to a different destination, they may need a transit visa, depending on the length of the layover and the country's transit policies. Some countries have exemptions or specific visa requirements for transit passengers.

It's important to note that visa requirements can change, so it's crucial for African migrants to consult the official government websites of the destination country's immigration authorities or contact the nearest embassy or consulate to obtain accurate and up-to-date information about visa requirements, application processes, and any supporting documentation needed. Working with immigration lawyers or authorized immigration consultants can also provide valuable guidance throughout the visa application process.

WORK PERMITS AND EMPLOYMENT-BASED IMMIGRATION

Many countries have specific programs and requirements for African migrants seeking employment opportunities. Work permits may be tied to specific job offers, skill shortages, or labor market demands. Some countries may have quotas or points-based systems to prioritize highly skilled or sought-after professionals.

Work permits and employment-based immigration programs are commonly used by countries to attract foreign workers with specific skills, expertise, or qualifications. These programs allow African migrants to seek employment opportunities and legally work in their destination country.

Here Are Some Key Aspects Of Work Permits And Employment-Based Immigration:

1. **Work Permit Categories**: Countries often have different categories of work permits, each with its own eligibility criteria and requirements. These categories may include skilled worker programs, temporary work permits, intra-company transfers, seasonal work programs, and more. Each category may have specific criteria related to education, work experience, language proficiency, and job offers from employers.

2. **Job Offers and Employer Sponsorship:** Many countries require African migrants to have a job offer from a local employer to be eligible for a work permit. The employer typically needs to demonstrate that they have made efforts to fill the position with a local candidate, but have been

unable to do so. The employer may need to provide supporting documents such as a labor market impact assessment or proof of their financial capacity.

3. **Skills Shortages and Labor Market Needs:** Some countries have specific programs that address skills shortages or labor market needs. These programs aim to attract foreign workers in occupations where there is a demand for skilled professionals. African migrants with qualifications, expertise, or experience in these occupations may have better chances of obtaining a work permit in such programs.

4. **Points-Based Systems:** Certain countries use points-based systems to assess the eligibility of foreign workers. Points are assigned based on factors such as education, language proficiency, work experience, age, and adaptability. African migrants who meet the required point threshold may be eligible to apply for a work permit or permanent residence.

5. **Duration and Renewal:** Work permits are typically issued for a specific duration, which can vary depending on the country and the specific program. After the initial period, the work permit may be renewable, subject to certain conditions,

such as maintaining employment, meeting residency requirements, and complying with immigration laws.

6. **Dependents and Family Sponsorship:** Work permits often include provisions for the sponsorship of accompanying family members. African migrants who hold a valid work permit may be able to bring their spouse, children, or other eligible family members to join them in the destination country. Each country has specific requirements regarding financial support, relationship verification, and documentation.

It's important for African migrants to thoroughly research the work permit options and requirements of their intended destination country. Official government websites, immigration authorities, and embassies or consulates can provide detailed information on work permit programs, application processes, and any changes to immigration policies. Consulting with immigration lawyers or authorized immigration consultants can also help navigate the complexities of work permits and employment-based immigration.

REFUGEE AND ASYLUM POLICIES

African migrants fleeing persecution, conflict, or other forms of harm may seek refugee status or apply for asylum in their destination country. Each country has its own procedures and criteria to assess and process asylum claims, considering factors like human rights abuses, political instability, and humanitarian crises.

Refugee and asylum policies are measures put in place by countries to address the needs of and protect individuals who have fled their home countries due to persecution, conflict, or violence. These policies aim to provide refuge and legal protection to those seeking safety and to ensure that their human rights are respected. While specific policies can vary from country to country, I can provide you with an overview of common elements and international frameworks related to refugee and asylum policies.

1. **Refugee Definition:** The definition of a refugee is crucial in determining who is eligible for protection. RdxThe internationally accepted definition of a A refugee is outlined in the 1951 Refugee Convention and its 1967 Protocol, which state that a refugee is a person who has a well-founded fear of persecution

based on race, religion, nationality, political opinion, or membership in a particular social group. Some countries may also consider other forms of harm, such as generalized violence or environmental disasters, in their asylum policies.

2. **Non-Refoulement Principle:** The principle of non-refoulement is a fundamental principle of international refugee law. It prohibits the return of refugees to a country where they may face persecution, torture, or other serious human rights violations. This principle is enshrined in various international human rights treaties and forms the cornerstone of refugee protection.

3. **Asylum Process:** Countries typically have established asylum procedures that determine how asylum claims are processed and assessed. These procedures may include application forms, interviews, and the examination of supporting evidence to determine if the person meets the criteria for refugee status.

4. **Burden-Sharing and Resettlement:** Due to the global nature of refugee movements, international Cooperation and burden-sharing are essential. Resettlement programs allow refugees who are unable to return to their home countries or integrate

into the first country of asylum to be relocated to a third country willing to provide them with permanent resettlement.

5. **Integration and Social Support:** Successful integration of refugees into host communities is crucial for their long-term well-being. Policies promoting access to education, healthcare, employment opportunities, language training, and social services help refugees rebuild their lives and contribute to the host society.

6. **Temporary Protection:** In some cases, countries may grant temporary protection to individuals fleeing conflict or other extraordinary circumstances. Temporary protection allows for immediate shelter and assistance until the situation in their home country stabilizes.

7. **Border Management and Detention:** Managing the movement of people across borders is an important aspect of refugee and asylum policies. Countries often establish border management procedures, including the possibility of detaining individuals who arrive without proper documentation. However, it is essential to ensure that detention practices are in line with human rights standards, particularly with regard to the

rights and well-being of children and vulnerable individuals

It's important to note that refugee and asylum policies can differ significantly from one country to another. National legislation, domestic politics, and regional dynamics play a role in shaping these policies. Additionally, global events, such as conflicts and humanitarian crises, may influence the approaches taken by different countries.

FAMILY REUNIFICATION

Immigration policies often include provisions for family reunification, allowing African migrants to join their family members who are already residing in the destination country. These policies typically have eligibility criteria, such as proving the relationship and meeting financial and accommodation requirements.

Family reunification is a key component of refugee and asylum policies in many countries. It refers to the process of reuniting separated family members who have been forced to flee their home countries and seek refuge in different locations. The principle of family unity recognizes the importance of maintaining family ties and provides a legal framework for the reunification of families in a safe and secure environment.

Here Are Some Important Aspects Of Family Reunification:

1. **Definition of Family:** Countries may have different definitions of family for the purpose of reunification. While spouses and minor children are typically included, some countries may also consider parents, siblings, or other dependent relatives as eligible family members.
2. **Eligibility Criteria:** Specific criteria are established to determine the eligibility for family reunification. These criteria may include proving the family relationship, demonstrating the refugee or asylum status of the person initiating the reunification, and meeting certain financial or accommodation requirements.
3. **Application Process:** The application process for family reunification typically involves submitting documentation and evidence to establish the family relationship and eligibility. The process may include filling out forms, providing identification

documents, and undergoing interviews or background checks.

4. **Processing Time:** The time taken to process family reunification applications can vary depending on the country and the volume of applications. Ideally, countries strive to process applications in a timely manner to minimize the separation of families.

5. **Priority Groups:** Some countries give priority to certain groups for family reunification, such as vulnerable individuals, unaccompanied minors, or those with urgent medical needs. This ensures that those in the most vulnerable situations are prioritized for reunification.

6. **Sponsorship Requirements:** In some cases, the person initiating the reunification (the sponsor) may be required to demonstrate their ability to provide financial support and accommodation for the family members being reunited.

7. **Integration Support:** Upon arrival, reunited family members may be provided with integrated support services to help them settle into the host country. These services can include language classes, access to education and healthcare, employment assistance, and social support networks.

It is important to note that family reunification policies can differ between countries, and the specific details and requirements may vary. It is advisable to consult the relevant immigration authorities or legal experts in the country in question to obtain accurate and up-to-date information on family reunification processes and requirements.

INTEGRATION AND PATHWAYS TO CITIZENSHIP

Countries may have integration programs to help African migrants adapt to their new society, learn the language, and access education, healthcare, and employment services. Policies related to pathways to citizenship determine the requirements and process for African migrants to obtain citizenship in the host country.

Integration and pathways to citizenship are essential components of refugee and asylum policies, aimed at facilitating the successful integration of refugees and asylum seekers into the host society and providing them with a secure legal status.

Here Are Some Key Aspects Related To Integration And Pathways To Citizenship:

INTEGRATION:

1. **Language and Education:** Access to language training programs and educational opportunities is crucial for refugees and asylum seekers to acquire language skills, gain education, and enhance their employability.

2. **Employment and Skills Training:** Policies promoting equal access to employment opportunities, vocational training, and skills development help refugees and asylum seekers secure sustainable livelihoods and contribute to the local economy.

3. **Housing and Social Services:** Adequate housing, healthcare services, and social support networks play a vital role in ensuring the well-being and integration of refugees and asylum seekers.

4. **Cultural Orientation and Community Engagement:** Providing cultural orientation programs and facilitating community engagement activities help newcomers understand the host country's culture, norms, and social systems, fostering social cohesion and mutual understanding.

5. **Anti-Discrimination and Equality:** Policies addressing discrimination and promoting equality are crucial to ensuring that refugees and asylum seekers have equal rights and opportunities in the host country.

PATHWAYS TO CITIZENSHIP:

1. **Asylum-Based Pathways:** In some cases, refugees who have been granted asylum may be eligible to apply for citizenship after meeting specific residency requirements, such as a certain number of years of continuous residence.
2. **Naturalization Processes:** Naturalization processes allow refugees and asylum seekers to acquire citizenship through an application process that typically involves demonstrating a certain period of residence, language proficiency, knowledge of the host country's laws and values, and meeting other requirements.
3. **Special Provisions:** Some countries may have special provisions or expedited pathways to citizenship for refugees and asylum seekers,

recognizing their unique circumstances and facilitating their integration.

4. **Dual Citizenship:** Some countries allow individuals to hold dual citizenship, enabling refugees and asylum seekers to retain their citizenship of origin while acquiring citizenship in the host country.

It's important to note that the specific pathways to citizenship and integration policies vary among countries. The legal frameworks, requirements, and processes are set by each nation's laws and regulations. It is recommended to consult the relevant immigration authorities or legal experts in the specific country to obtain accurate and up-to-date information on integration programs and pathways to citizenship.

TEMPORARY PROTECTED STATUS

In certain situations, such as natural disasters, armed conflicts, or humanitarian crises, countries may offer temporary protected status to African migrants already residing in their territory. This allows them to stay temporarily and protects them from deportation until the situation in their home country improves.

Temporary Protected Status (TPS) is a temporary immigration status granted to eligible individuals who are unable to safely return to their home countries due to ongoing armed conflict, environmental disasters, or other extraordinary and temporary conditions. TPS allows individuals to remain in a host country for a designated period, during which they are protected from deportation and may receive work authorization.

Here Are Some Key Aspects Of Temporary Protected Status:

1. **Eligibility:** Eligibility for TPS is determined by the host country's government. Generally, individuals must meet certain criteria, such as being a national of a designated country, being physically present in the host country during a specified period, and demonstrating continuous residence in the host country since a designated date.
2. **Designation and Termination:** The host country's government designates countries for TPS based on specific conditions, such as armed conflict,

natural disasters, or other extraordinary circumstances. TPS is typically granted for a specific time period. However, TPS designations can be terminated if the conditions in the home country improve and are deemed safe for the return of its nationals.

3.   **Benefits and Protections:** While under TPS, individuals are protected from deportation and can obtain work authorization, allowing them to support themselves and their families. TPS beneficiaries may also be eligible for certain public benefits, such as access to healthcare and education.

4.   **Renewal and Extension:** TPS status is not automatically renewed. Individuals with TPS must reapply during designated registration periods to maintain their status. Depending on the situation in their home country, the host country's government may decide to extend TPS for eligible individuals.

5.   **Travel Authorization:** TPS beneficiaries may be eligible to obtain travel authorization to temporarily leave the host country and return without forfeiting their TPS status. However, it is important to adhere to the specific rules and procedures related to travel authorization to avoid jeopardizing TPS benefits.

6.   **Path to Permanent Residence:** TPS, by itself, does not provide a direct pathway to permanent residence or citizenship. However, individuals with TPS may be eligible to pursue other forms of legal status or immigration benefits through alternative immigration pathways available to them.

It is important to note that TPS policies and procedures can vary between host countries. The details of eligibility requirements, benefits, and application processes are determined by the laws and regulations of the specific country granting TPS. It is advisable to consult the relevant immigration authorities or legal experts in the host country for accurate and up-to-date information on TPS.

CHAPTER 3

HUMAN RIGHTS AND TREATMENT OF MIGRANTS

The treatment of African migrants in other countries has raised concerns about human rights abuses and exploitation. It is important to discuss ways to ensure that migrants are treated fairly and with dignity, and how to address issues such as detention, deportation, and exploitation.

The protection of human rights and the fair treatment of migrants are fundamental principles that should be upheld by all countries. Migrants, regardless of their immigration status, are entitled to the same basic human rights and dignity as any other individual.

Key Aspects Related To Human Rights And The Treatment Of Migrants:

NON-DISCRIMINATION

Migrants should be treated without discrimination based on their race, nationality, ethnicity, gender, religion, or any other protected characteristic. Equal protection under the law and access to basic services and rights should be ensured for all migrants.

In today's globalized world, the movement of people across borders has become a defining feature of our societies. In this context, ensuring non-discrimination against migrants is not just a moral imperative but a fundamental human rights obligation. Every individual, regardless of their immigration or migrant status, deserves to be treated with dignity, equality, and respect.

Non-discrimination of migrants encompasses a range of principles and practices aimed at protecting their rights. It means that migrants should have equal access to basic services, such as education, healthcare, and housing, without facing discrimination based on their nationality or migrant status. It also means that migrants should be entitled to fair and just treatment in the workplace, with access to decent work conditions, fair wages, and the ability to exercise their labor rights.

Beyond equal treatment, non-discrimination entails challenging xenophobic attitudes and stereotypes that perpetuate exclusion and marginalization. It involves promoting social integration by facilitating language training, cultural exchange, and community participation opportunities for migrants. Governments, civil society organizations, and individuals must work collectively to foster inclusive societies that recognize and celebrate the contributions of migrants.

Addressing discrimination against migrants requires comprehensive legal frameworks, robust policies, and public awareness campaigns. It demands proactive measures to combat hate crimes, hate speech, and xenophobia targeting migrants. By promoting respect for diversity and fostering a culture of inclusion, we can create societies that uphold the principles of equality and non-discrimination.

In the pursuit of non-discrimination of migrants, we not only protect the rights of individuals but also strengthen our societies. By embracing the values of equality, we build bridges across cultures, promote social cohesion, and create a brighter future for all. Let us stand united in rejecting discrimination and championing the rights and dignity of every migrant who seeks a better life within our borders.

RIGHT TO LIFE AND SECURITY

Migrants have the right to life and security. This includes protection from violence, torture, cruel or inhumane treatment, and arbitrary detention. Governments should ensure the safety and well-being of migrants within their territories.

The right to life and security is an inherent human right that must be protected and upheld for all individuals, including African migrants. As they embark on perilous journeys in search of safety and a better future, it is crucial to ensure that their lives are safeguarded and their security is guaranteed.

African migrants often face numerous challenges and vulnerabilities along their migration routes. They are exposed to risks such as human trafficking, exploitation, violence, and discrimination. To protect their right to life, it is imperative that governments, international organizations, and civil society collaborate to address these pressing issues.

Firstly, combating human trafficking and smuggling networks is paramount. These criminal activities put the lives of African migrants at great risk. Strengthening border controls, increasing cooperation between countries, and providing support to victims are essential steps in combating this abhorrent trade.

Secondly, addressing the root causes that force African migrants to embark on dangerous journeys is vital. Investing in development initiatives, poverty reduction, and conflict resolution in their countries of origin can alleviate the push factors driving migration and provide better opportunities for individuals to flourish in their homelands.

Thirdly, enhancing the legal pathways for migration, such as expanding avenues for family reunification, labor migration, and access to asylum, can provide African migrants with safer and more secure options. It is crucial to ensure that migration policies prioritize the protection of human rights and offer viable alternatives to irregular and dangerous migration routes.

Furthermore, promoting integration and inclusion of African migrants in destination countries is essential for their security and well-being. Access to education, healthcare, housing, and employment opportunities can empower migrants, enhance their socio-economic integration, and mitigate the risks they face.

In conclusion, protecting the right to life and security of African migrants requires comprehensive efforts that address both the immediate dangers they face during their journeys and the underlying causes that drive migration. By implementing proactive measures, fostering international cooperation, and upholding human rights principles, we can create a world where African migrants are respected, their lives are preserved, and their security is assured.

RIGHT TO SEEK ASYLUM

Migrants who are fleeing persecution or serious human rights violations have the right to seek asylum. They should be given the opportunity to present their asylum claims and have access to a fair and efficient asylum process.
The right to seek asylum is a fundamental human right enshrined in international law, and it holds significant importance for African migrants fleeing persecution, violence, and instability in their home countries. As they seek safety and protection, it is crucial to recognize and uphold their right to seek asylum.

African migrants often face dire circumstances, including political repression, armed conflict, and human rights abuses, prompting them to embark on perilous journeys in search of sanctuary. The right to seek asylum allows them to

Efforts should be made to reunite separated migrant children with their families through family tracing and reunification processes. In cases where family reunification is not possible, suitable alternative care arrangements should be provided, emphasizing the child's best interests.

Access to legal assistance is crucial to safeguard the rights of African migrant children. They should have access to legal representation and guidance throughout immigration and asylum processes, ensuring their voices are heard and their rights are protected.

International cooperation is vital in addressing the unique challenges faced by African migrant children. Collaboration between countries of origin, transit, and destination can facilitate the sharing of good practices, knowledge, and resources to ensure the effective protection of their rights.

In conclusion, ensuring the rights of African migrant children requires a comprehensive and child-centered approach. By prioritizing their access to education, healthcare, protection, and legal assistance, we can empower these children to thrive, contribute, and build a better future for themselves and their communities. It is through these efforts that we demonstrate our commitment to human rights and create a world where every child, regardless of their migration status, is given the opportunity to reach their full potential.

DETENTION AND ALTERNATIVES

If migrants are detained, it should be used as a measure of last resort and in accordance with international standards. Detention should be for the shortest period possible, and alternatives to detention should be explored whenever possible, particularly for vulnerable individuals, families, and children.

Detention of African migrants has been a contentious issue, raising concerns about human rights violations and the negative impact on individuals' well-being. It is crucial to prioritize alternatives to detention that respect the rights and dignity of African migrants while ensuring effective migration management.

Detention should be a measure of last resort and used only when absolutely necessary, with a clear legal basis and proportionality. African migrants, including children and families, should not be subjected to arbitrary or indefinite detention. Detention should be strictly time-limited and regularly reviewed, with access to legal counsel and effective remedies.

Implementing viable alternatives to detention is essential in promoting a rights-based approach to migration. Community-based alternatives, such as case management, reporting obligations, and community housing, offer effective solutions that balance migration management objectives with respect for human rights. These alternatives allow individuals to live in the community, maintain their dignity, and contribute to society while their immigration cases are processed.

Investing in comprehensive screening processes, risk assessments, and support services can facilitate the identification of vulnerable individuals who may require specialized assistance and protection, rather than being subjected to detention.

International cooperation is crucial in addressing the complexities of migration and ensuring the effective implementation of alternatives to detention. Sharing best practices, experiences, and resources can contribute to the development of comprehensive and sustainable alternatives that prioritize human rights and dignity.

In conclusion, detention should be a measure of last resort for African migrants, and alternatives should be explored and implemented whenever possible. By embracing community-based alternatives, promoting effective screening processes, and fostering international cooperation, we can uphold the human rights and dignity of African migrants while ensuring responsible and effective migration management. It is through these efforts that we can build more inclusive and compassionate societies that recognize the value and contributions of migrants.

INTEGRATION AND SOCIAL SERVICES

Migrants should have access to social services, such as healthcare, education, and social welfare, on an equal basis with the host population. Integration policies and support should be in place to facilitate the inclusion of migrants in the host society.

Integration plays a pivotal role in ensuring the successful inclusion of African migrants into their host societies. It is imperative to recognize the importance of providing adequate social services and support to facilitate their integration, fostering a cohesive and harmonious multicultural society.

African migrants bring diverse backgrounds, skills, and experiences, enriching the social fabric of their host communities. Investing in their integration not only benefits individuals but also contributes to the economic, social, and cultural development of the receiving countries.

Access to social services, including healthcare, education, housing, and employment opportunities, is crucial for African migrants' successful integration. Governments should prioritize the provision of these services, ensuring they are culturally sensitive, inclusive, and tailored to the unique needs of migrants.

Language acquisition programs and cultural orientation initiatives can help African migrants overcome linguistic and cultural barriers, enabling them to actively participate in their new communities. These programs foster mutual understanding, respect, and appreciation for diversity.

Promoting inclusive policies and combating discrimination are essential in creating an environment that embraces diversity and supports African migrants' integration. Anti-discrimination laws, diversity training, and awareness campaigns can challenge stereotypes, prejudices, and biases, fostering a more inclusive and tolerant society.

Collaboration between governments, civil society organizations, and migrant communities is crucial in facilitating integration. Establishing platforms for dialogue, consultation, and active participation of African migrants in decision-making processes can ensure their voices are heard, their concerns are addressed, and their contributions are recognized.

In conclusion, promoting integration and providing adequate social services to African migrants are essential for building inclusive, cohesive, and prosperous societies. By investing in their integration, embracing diversity, and fostering a culture of inclusivity, we can empower African migrants to thrive, contribute, and participate fully in their host communities. Together, we can create a future where diversity is celebrated, barriers are overcome, and the potential of every individual, regardless of their migration background, is realized.

It is important to note that while these principles and rights exist, the actual treatment of migrants can vary among countries and be influenced by various factors, including national laws, policies, and public attitudes. International human rights standards and frameworks, such as the Universal Declaration of Human Rights and international conventions, provide guidance for the protection of the rights of migrants. Efforts should be made by governments, civil society, and international organizations to promote and ensure the human rights and fair treatment of migrants.

CHAPTER 4

ECONOMIC IMPACTS

African migration can have economic impacts on both the countries of origin and destination. It is important to explore the economic effects of migration, including remittances, brain drain, and the impact on local labor markets.

African migration has significant economic impacts on both the countries of origin and destination. While the economic effects can vary depending on factors such as the skill level of migrants, the sectors they work in, and the policies in place, African migration generally contributes to economic growth and development in several ways.

REMITTANCES

African migrants working abroad often send money back to their families in their home countries, which has a substantial impact on the local economies. Remittances can contribute to household consumption, poverty reduction, and investment in education, healthcare, and businesses, stimulating economic activities in the countries of origin.

Remittances from African migrants play a significant role in the economies of their home countries, providing a vital source of income and contributing to economic development in various ways.

Here Are Some Key Aspects Of Remittances From African Migrants:

1. **Economic Support:** Remittances are a lifeline for many African families, particularly in regions with high levels of poverty and limited economic opportunities. The funds received from migrant family members abroad help to cover basic needs, such as food, housing, education, and healthcare, improving the living standards of recipient households.

2. **Poverty Reduction:** Remittances have a direct impact on poverty reduction by providing financial stability and helping recipient families meet their immediate needs. They can alleviate poverty in rural areas and disadvantaged communities, where access to formal financial services may be limited.

3. **Investment and Entrepreneurship:** Remittances often serve as capital for small-scale business ventures and entrepreneurial activities. Migrant families may invest remittance funds in local businesses, agriculture, or real estate, stimulating economic growth and job creation. This can contribute to the development of local industries and provide opportunities for others in the community.

4. **Education and Skills Development:** Remittances enable families to invest in education and skills training for their children. This investment in human capital helps to break the cycle of poverty, as educated individuals are more likely to secure better job opportunities and contribute to the economic growth of their communities and countries.

5. **Financial Sector Development:** The influx of remittances can also contribute to the development of formal financial systems in African countries. Financial institutions may develop products and services tailored to migrants and their families, encouraging financial inclusion and promoting economic stability.

6. **Macroeconomic Stability:** Remittances can have a positive impact on a country's balance of payments,

foreign exchange reserves, and overall macroeconomic stability. They can help reduce external debt, strengthen the local currency, and provide a buffer during times of economic volatility or external shocks.

However, it is important to note that there are challenges associated with remittances, such as high transaction costs, limited financial literacy, and potential dependence on external income sources. Governments and financial institutions should work towards reducing barriers, promoting financial literacy, and creating an enabling environment for productive use of remittances to maximize their impact on economic development.

In conclusion, remittances from African migrants play a crucial role in supporting families, reducing poverty, stimulating entrepreneurship, and contributing to economic development. By recognizing the significance of remittances and implementing policies to harness their potential, African countries can leverage this valuable resource for sustainable and inclusive growth.

LABOR MARKET CONTRIBUTIONS

African migrants fill important gaps in the labor markets of destination countries. They often work in sectors with labor shortages, such as healthcare, agriculture, construction, and hospitality. Their contribution helps to sustain and expand these industries, creating job opportunities and driving economic growth.

African migrants make substantial contributions to labor markets in both their host countries and countries of origin. Their participation in various industries and sectors has significant economic impacts.

Here Are Some Key Aspects Of Their Labor Market Contributions:

1. **Filling Labor Market Gaps:** African migrants often fill labor shortages in their host countries, particularly in sectors where there is a demand for workers. They contribute to industries such as healthcare, agriculture, construction, hospitality, and domestic work. Their presence helps to address skill gaps and meet the demand for labor, supporting the growth and sustainability of these sectors.

2. **Job Creation:** African migrant entrepreneurs play a crucial role in job creation. Many migrants start their own businesses, which generate employment opportunities for both fellow migrants and local communities. These businesses contribute to economic growth, promote diversity, and foster innovation and entrepreneurship in their host countries.

3. **Economic Productivity:** African migrants bring diverse skills, knowledge, and experiences to their host countries' labor markets. They often possess expertise in various fields, including science, technology, engineering, medicine, and finance. Their contributions enhance productivity, drive innovation, and contribute to the overall competitiveness of the economies in which they work.

4. **Skills Transfer and Knowledge Exchange:** Highly skilled African migrants contribute to knowledge transfer and skills development in their host countries. They bring expertise and experiences from their home countries and have the potential to enhance local industries and institutions. Through their interactions with local professionals and collaboration with research and academic

institutions, they contribute to the exchange of ideas and the transfer of knowledge.

5. **Diversity and Cultural Enrichment:** African migrants contribute to the diversity and cultural richness of the labor force in their host countries. Their diverse backgrounds, languages, and traditions bring fresh perspectives, fostering a multicultural work environment. This cultural exchange can enhance creativity, problem-solving, and cross-cultural understanding among workers.

6. **Remittances and Economic Impact:** African migrants who are employed in host countries often send remittances to their families in their countries of origin. These financial flows have a positive impact on the local economies, supporting household consumption, investment in education and healthcare, and the growth of small businesses. Remittances contribute to poverty reduction, stimulate local economies, and promote economic stability.

In conclusion, African migrants make significant contributions to labor markets in their host countries, filling skill gaps, driving economic productivity, promoting entrepreneurship, and enhancing cultural diversity. Their labor market contributions have positive economic impacts, supporting job creation, knowledge transfer, and overall economic growth. Recognizing and valuing these contributions is crucial for creating inclusive and thriving societies that benefit from the talents and skills of migrants.

ENTREPRENEURSHIP AND INNOVATION

Many African migrants are entrepreneurial and start businesses in their host countries. These enterprises generate employment, create economic value, and contribute to innovation and diversification of local economies. African migrant entrepreneurs bring unique skills, cultural knowledge, and business networks, enriching the business landscape in their destination countries.
African migrants have a strong entrepreneurial spirit and make notable contributions to entrepreneurship and innovation in their host countries. They bring with them diverse skills, experiences, and cultural perspectives that enrich the business landscape.

Here Are Some Key Aspects Of Their Entrepreneurship And Innovation:

1. **Business Creation:** African migrants often establish their own businesses in their host countries. These ventures span a wide range of industries, including retail, hospitality, construction, healthcare, technology, and creative arts. Their entrepreneurial endeavors create job opportunities, stimulate economic growth, and contribute to the overall business ecosystem.

2. **Market Niche Identification:** African migrants often identify unique market niches and fill gaps in the local economy. They leverage their knowledge of both the host country and their country of origin to meet the demands of specific communities or cultural groups. This allows them to provide tailored products and services that cater to diverse consumer needs, fostering economic diversity and consumer satisfaction.

3. **Cultural Diversity and Innovation:** African migrant entrepreneurs bring cultural diversity and innovative approaches to their businesses. They introduce new products, services, and business models that reflect their cultural heritage, catering to diverse customer preferences and expanding consumer choices. This infusion of cultural diversity

fosters creativity, innovation, and entrepreneurship in the host country.

4. **Job Creation and Economic Growth:** African migrant entrepreneurs play a significant role in job creation. They establish businesses that employ not only themselves but also local residents. By generating employment opportunities, they contribute to reducing unemployment rates, fostering economic growth, and stimulating local economies.

5. **Knowledge and Skills Transfer:** African migrant entrepreneurs bring valuable knowledge and skills from their home countries. They may introduce unique production techniques, business practices, or market insights that contribute to innovation and efficiency in their industries. Their interactions with local professionals and collaborations can lead to knowledge and skills transfer, benefiting the overall business environment.

6. **Social Impact:** African migrant entrepreneurs often demonstrate a commitment to social impact and community development. They initiate projects and initiatives that address social challenges, such as education, healthcare, poverty, and sustainable development, both in their host countries and

countries of origin. Their businesses serve as agents of positive change, contributing to the well-being of communities and fostering social cohesion.

In conclusion, African migrant entrepreneurs bring innovative ideas, cultural diversity, and a strong work ethic to their host countries' business landscapes. Their entrepreneurial endeavors have a positive impact on job creation, economic growth, knowledge transfer, and social development. Supporting and promoting their entrepreneurship and innovation can unlock their full potential, benefiting both the migrants themselves and the societies in which they reside.

SKILLS AND KNOWLEDGE TRANSFER

Highly skilled African migrants contribute to the knowledge and skills pool in their host countries. They bring expertise in various sectors, including science, technology, engineering, and medicine. Their knowledge transfer and participation in research and development activities contribute to the growth and competitiveness of host country industries.

African migrants bring valuable skills, knowledge, and experiences to their host countries, contributing to skills transfer and knowledge exchange. Their expertise acquired from their home countries can positively impact the economies, industries, and communities they join.

Here Are Some Key Aspects Of Skills And Knowledge Transfer By African Migrants:

1. **Professional Expertise:** Highly skilled African migrants, including doctors, engineers, scientists, academics, and professionals in various fields, bring specialized knowledge and expertise to their host countries. They contribute to research and development, innovation, and the advancement of industries, strengthening the local workforce and enhancing productivity.

2. **Entrepreneurial Skills:** African migrants often possess strong entrepreneurial skills gained through their experiences and cultural backgrounds. They introduce innovative business models, management practices, and market insights, fostering entrepreneurial spirit and contributing to the growth of local businesses and industries.

3. **Cultural Diversity and Intercultural Competence:** African migrants bring cultural diversity and intercultural competence to their host

countries. Their experiences and perspectives promote cross-cultural understanding, tolerance, and cooperation. This cultural exchange enhances creativity, problem-solving, and the ability to navigate diverse environments, benefiting both the migrants and the host communities.

4. **Knowledge Exchange:** African migrants engage in knowledge exchange with local professionals, academics, and researchers, fostering collaboration and the transfer of ideas. They participate in conferences, seminars, and academic programs, sharing their expertise and contributing to intellectual development in their fields.

5. **Language and Communication Skills:** Many African migrants are multilingual, speaking their native languages as well as the languages of their host countries. This linguistic proficiency facilitates communication and cultural understanding between diverse communities. Language skills acquired by migrants can also benefit local businesses and industries by opening up new markets and facilitating international connections.

6. **Community Development:** African migrants often play an active role in community development initiatives. They share their skills and knowledge by

volunteering, mentoring, or providing training programs to empower local communities. This involvement strengthens social cohesion and promotes inclusive growth.

7. **Return Migration and Brain Gain:** Some African migrants eventually return to their home countries, bringing back acquired skills, experiences, and networks. This "brain gain" contributes to the development of local industries, entrepreneurship, and knowledge-based economies, creating opportunities for sustainable growth.

In conclusion, African migrants' skills and knowledge transfer contribute significantly to the host countries' economic, social, and cultural development. Recognizing and harnessing their expertise, promoting collaboration, and creating supportive environments for integration can maximize the positive impact of skills and knowledge transfer, benefiting both the migrants and the host communities.

TRADE AND INVESTMENT

African migrants often facilitate trade and investment between their home countries and their host countries. They act as intermediaries, connecting businesses and fostering economic cooperation. They also contribute to foreign direct investment by investing in businesses and industries in both the countries of origin and destination.

African migrants play a crucial role in facilitating trade and investment between their host countries and their countries of origin. Their economic activities contribute to bilateral trade, foreign direct investment, and overall economic development.

Here Are Some Key Aspects Of The Trade And Investment Activities Of African Migrants:

1. **Market Linkages:** African migrants often act as intermediaries, connecting businesses and fostering trade relationships between their host countries and their countries of origin. They have cultural knowledge, language skills, and business networks that enable them to identify market opportunities and facilitate trade in goods and services.

2. **Remittances as Investment:** African migrants frequently invest a portion of their earnings in businesses, real estate, and other economic activities in their home countries. These remittances

contribute to domestic investment and stimulate local economies, supporting job creation and economic growth.

3. **Diaspora Investments:** African migrants form part of the African diaspora, which has a significant impact on investment in the region. They invest in various sectors, such as agriculture, manufacturing, infrastructure, and technology. Diaspora investments can lead to capital inflows, technology transfer, and the development of local industries.

4. **Knowledge and Skills Transfer:** African migrants bring expertise, knowledge, and industry-specific skills from their host countries. This transfer of knowledge can enhance local industries, improve production processes, and promote innovation in their countries of origin. Migrants often engage in capacity-building initiatives, training programs, and knowledge exchange, benefiting local businesses and contributing to economic development.

5. **Foreign Direct Investment (FDI):** African migrants who have established successful businesses abroad may choose to invest in their countries of origin. They bring FDI, which can create employment opportunities, transfer technology and

management practices, and stimulate economic growth in key sectors.

6. **Cultural Exchanges and Tourism:** African migrants act as ambassadors, promoting cultural exchanges and tourism between their host countries and their countries of origin. They facilitate the flow of tourists, encourage business collaborations, and showcase the rich cultural heritage and tourism potential of their home countries. This contributes to revenue generation, job creation, and economic development in the tourism sector.

7. **Networking and Business Partnerships:** African migrants often establish business networks and partnerships in their host countries. These connections can lead to joint ventures, trade agreements, and investment opportunities that benefit both the host country and the country of origin. Collaboration between migrants and local businesses fosters economic cooperation and mutually beneficial relationships.

In conclusion, African migrants play a significant role in trade and investment, connecting markets, facilitating remittances, and promoting economic development. Their contributions enhance bilateral trade, stimulate investment, foster knowledge and skills transfer, and promote cultural exchange. Recognizing the potential of African migrants as agents of trade and investment can unlock opportunities for inclusive growth and sustainable development in both their host countries and their countries of origin.

African migration has positive economic impacts on both the countries of origin and destination. Remittances, labor market contributions, entrepreneurship, skills transfer, and trade and investment are among the key ways in which African migration stimulates economic growth, reduces poverty, and fosters development. It is important for policymakers to recognize and harness these economic benefits while ensuring that migrants' rights are protected and their integration is supported for mutual prosperity.

CHAPTER 5

INTEGRATION AND SOCIAL COHESION

Integrating migrants into a new society can be challenging, and it is important to discuss ways to promote social cohesion and ensure that migrants are able to fully participate in their new communities.

Integration and social cohesion are essential for the successful inclusion of African migrants into their host societies. When migrants are integrated, they can contribute fully to the social, economic, and cultural fabric of their new communities.

Here Are Some Key Aspects Of Integration And Social Cohesion Of African Migrants:

LANGUAGE ACQUISITION

Learning the local language is crucial for effective communication, accessing education and job opportunities, and fostering social connections. African migrants who

potential of African migrants to contribute positively to the social, economic, and cultural development of their new home.

EDUCATION AND SKILLS DEVELOPMENT

Access to quality education and skills development programs is vital for the integration of African migrants. Equipping migrants with language skills, vocational training, and education that aligns with local labor market needs enhances their employment prospects and social mobility, enabling them to contribute meaningfully to the host society.

Education and skills development play a vital role in empowering African migrants to contribute fully to their new communities and realize their potential.

Access to quality education equips African migrants with the necessary knowledge, skills, and qualifications to actively participate in the social, economic, and cultural aspects of their new community. It provides them with a foundation for personal and professional growth, enabling them to secure better employment opportunities and contribute to the local economy.

Education enhances language proficiency, facilitating effective communication and integration. It enables migrants to learn the language of their host country, which is crucial for establishing connections, accessing services, and engaging in meaningful interactions with locals. Language proficiency broadens their social networks, helps them understand local customs and values, and fosters a sense of belonging.

Skills development programs equip African migrants with industry-specific skills, vocational training, and professional certifications aligned with local labor market needs. This enhances their employability and enables them to fill skill gaps within the community. By acquiring relevant skills, migrants can contribute to economic growth, entrepreneurship, and innovation in their new community.

Education and skill development also foster cultural exchange and understanding. African migrants bring their diverse backgrounds, experiences, and perspectives to the learning environment, enriching the educational experience for both themselves and their peers. This exchange of knowledge and ideas promotes mutual respect, tolerance, and appreciation of different cultures, strengthening social cohesion.

Furthermore, education empowers African migrants to actively participate in community development initiatives, volunteer work, and civic engagement. By leveraging their education and skills, migrants can contribute to community projects, mentor others, and actively engage in decision-making processes. This active involvement strengthens their sense of belonging and facilitates their integration into the community.

In summary, education and skills development play a pivotal role in enabling African migrants to contribute fully to their new communities. They provide migrants with the necessary tools, knowledge, and qualifications to participate in the social, economic, and cultural aspects of their host society. By investing in education and skills development programs, communities can harness the talents and potential of African migrants, fostering their integration and creating inclusive environments where everyone can thrive.

EMPLOYMENT AND ECONOMIC INTEGRATION

Providing equal employment opportunities for African migrants promotes their economic integration. Recognizing their qualifications, skills, and professional experiences ensures they have fair access to job markets. Supportive policies, job placement services, and recognition of foreign credentials can facilitate their integration into the labor force.

Employment and economic integration play a crucial role in empowering African migrants to contribute fully to their new communities and achieve economic self-sufficiency.

Securing employment is essential for African migrants as it provides them with a stable source of income, enhances their financial independence, and facilitates their integration into the local economy. By being employed, migrants can actively contribute to the economic growth of their host community.

Economic integration allows African migrants to utilize their skills, knowledge, and experiences, filling labor market gaps and contributing to the development of various sectors. Migrants bring diverse perspectives, cultural insights, and innovative ideas that can enhance productivity, competitiveness, and entrepreneurship in their new community.

Employment opportunities enable African migrants to build social networks, establish connections, and forge relationships with locals and other community members. Through their workplace interactions, they can foster understanding, cultural exchange, and mutual respect, contributing to social cohesion and building bridges between different communities.

Economic integration also reduces dependence on social welfare systems, as migrants become self-reliant and contribute to tax revenues. This, in turn, benefits the wider community by relieving the burden on public resources and enabling investment in social services, infrastructure, and community development initiatives.

Furthermore, economic integration enhances the overall diversity and inclusivity of the local labor market. By embracing the skills and talents of African migrants, host communities can tap into a broader talent pool, fostering innovation, creativity, and competitiveness.

To promote employment and economic integration, it is essential to address potential barriers such as discrimination, unequal access to job opportunities, and recognition of foreign qualifications. Implementing inclusive policies, providing language and skills training, and supporting entrepreneurship initiatives can facilitate the successful economic integration of African migrants.

In summary, employment and economic integration are instrumental in empowering African migrants to contribute fully to their new communities. By recognizing their skills, creating equal employment opportunities, and fostering an inclusive and supportive environment, host communities can benefit from the diverse talents, experiences, and contributions of African migrants, leading to shared prosperity and social cohesion.

SOCIAL SUPPORT AND COMMUNITY ENGAGEMENT

Establishing support networks and community organizations specifically focused on the needs of African migrants helps foster social cohesion. These platforms provide guidance, counseling, and resources to migrants, enabling them to navigate the challenges of integration. Encouraging participation in community events, volunteer work, and cultural exchanges strengthens social connections and mutual understanding.

Social support networks and community engagement are essential for African migrants as they navigate the challenges of settling into a new community. These factors provide a sense of belonging, empowerment, and connection that enable migrants to contribute fully to their new communities.

Social support networks offer practical assistance, guidance, and emotional support to African migrants. They help migrants access information about housing, healthcare, education, and other essential services. Social support networks also provide a platform for sharing experiences, addressing challenges, and fostering social connections with fellow migrants and community members.

Community engagement provides opportunities for African migrants to actively participate in community activities, initiatives, and events. By engaging in volunteer work, cultural exchanges, and community projects, migrants can contribute their skills, talents, and cultural diversity to the betterment of the community. This active involvement fosters a sense of ownership, mutual respect, and understanding between migrants and the host community.

Social support and community engagement initiatives also empower African migrants to advocate for their rights, needs, and interests. By providing platforms for dialogue, representation, and collective action, migrants can address issues of discrimination, xenophobia, and social exclusion. This engagement not only benefits migrants themselves but also promotes social cohesion and inclusivity within the broader community.

Additionally, social support networks and community engagement contribute to the overall well-being of African migrants. They help alleviate feelings of isolation, loneliness, and cultural disorientation often experienced during the integration process. By nurturing a supportive environment, these initiatives enhance migrants' mental health, self-confidence, and resilience, enabling them to actively contribute to their new community.

In summary, social support networks and community engagement are vital in facilitating the full integration and contribution of African migrants. By providing practical assistance, fostering social connections, and promoting active participation, host communities can harness the talents, skills, and cultural diversity of African migrants, leading to social cohesion, cultural enrichment, and shared prosperity.

ANTI-DISCRIMINATION AND DIVERSITY POLICIES

Implementing policies that combat discrimination, racism, and xenophobia is crucial for promoting social cohesion. Creating an inclusive and welcoming environment for African migrants involves raising awareness, educating the public, and enforcing anti-discrimination laws. Embracing diversity and celebrating cultural differences fosters a sense of belonging for migrants and enhances social cohesion.

Anti-discrimination and diversity policies are essential in ensuring equal treatment, protection, and opportunities for African migrants in their new communities. These policies aim to eliminate prejudice, bias, and systemic barriers that may hinder migrants' full participation and contribution.

By implementing anti-discrimination policies, host communities can create a welcoming environment that respects the rights and dignity of African migrants. These policies promote equal access to employment, housing, education, healthcare, and other essential services, regardless of a person's ethnic background or migration status. This ensures that migrants have a fair chance to contribute their skills, knowledge, and experiences to the community.

Diversity policies recognize and embrace the richness of African migrants' cultural, linguistic, and social diversity. They promote respect, tolerance, and inclusion of different backgrounds, fostering a sense of belonging and valuing the contributions of migrants to the community. By celebrating diversity, these policies encourage the exchange of ideas, perspectives, and experiences, leading to cultural enrichment and innovation.

Anti-discrimination and diversity policies also address the intersectional challenges faced by African migrant women, children, and vulnerable individuals. They ensure that specific needs and rights are protected, empowering these groups to contribute fully and actively participate in community life.

Furthermore, anti-discrimination and diversity policies send a powerful message about the values of equality, social justice, and human rights. They contribute to building a community that stands against discrimination, xenophobia, and prejudice, promoting social cohesion and harmony.

To maximize the impact of these policies, it is crucial to raise awareness, provide cultural sensitivity training, and encourage dialogue between migrants and the host community. By fostering understanding, empathy, and acceptance, anti-discrimination and diversity policies create an environment where African migrants can fully express their potential, talents, and contributions.

In summary, anti-discrimination and diversity policies are essential in creating an inclusive and supportive environment for African migrants to contribute fully to their new communities. By promoting equal treatment, celebrating diversity, and addressing systemic barriers, these policies foster a sense of belonging, respect, and social cohesion. Implementing and upholding these policies reflects a commitment to creating a just and inclusive society that benefits both African migrants and the broader community.

INTERCULTURAL EXCHANGE AND DIALOGUE

Encouraging intercultural exchange and dialogue between African migrants and the host community promotes understanding, tolerance, and appreciation of different cultures. Cultural events, festivals, and community programs that showcase African traditions, music, food, and art help break down stereotypes and build bridges between communities.

Intercultural exchange and dialogue play a pivotal role in facilitating the full contribution of African migrants to a new community. When migrants and the host community engage in meaningful interactions, share experiences, and foster understanding, it leads to social cohesion, integration, and mutual respect.

Intercultural exchange provides an opportunity for African migrants to share their rich cultural heritage, traditions, and perspectives with the host community. Through cultural events, festivals, workshops, and community initiatives, migrants can showcase their diverse talents, cuisine, arts, and music, promoting cultural diversity and fostering appreciation among the host community. This intercultural exchange helps to break down stereotypes, build bridges between different cultures, and create a sense of belonging for migrants.

Furthermore, dialogue between migrants and the host community encourages the exchange of ideas, knowledge, and experiences. It enables open discussions on various topics such as social norms, values, and traditions, allowing for a deeper understanding of each other's backgrounds and fostering empathy. Through dialogue, both parties can learn from one another, challenge preconceptions, and develop a shared sense of community.

Intercultural exchange and dialogue also contribute to the development of inclusive policies and practices. When migrants have a platform to express their needs, aspirations, and challenges, it enables policymakers and service providers to tailor their programs and services accordingly. It promotes the integration of migrants into the social, economic, and political fabric of the new community, ensuring their voices are heard and their contributions are recognized.

In conclusion, intercultural exchange and dialogue create opportunities for African migrants to contribute fully to a new community. By fostering understanding, appreciation of diversity, and meaningful interactions, intercultural exchange and dialogue enhance social cohesion, integration, and mutual respect. They provide a foundation for inclusive policies, empower migrants to share their talents and perspectives, and enable them to actively participate in shaping their new community.

HOUSING AND NEIGHBORHOOD INTEGRATION

Ensuring affordable and adequate housing options for African migrants facilitates their integration into neighborhoods and communities. Promoting mixed-income neighborhoods and avoiding the concentration of migrants in specific areas fosters social interaction, reduces isolation, and encourages integration.

Access to suitable and affordable housing is essential for African migrants as they settle into their new communities. Adequate housing provides stability, security, and a foundation for migrants to fully engage and contribute.

By ensuring equitable access to housing, host communities can create an environment where African migrants can establish a sense of belonging. Affordable housing options enable migrants to allocate their resources to other essential needs and contribute more actively to the local economy.

Moreover, neighborhood integration plays a pivotal role in fostering social connections and community engagement. When African migrants are integrated into diverse neighborhoods, they have opportunities to interact with local residents, learn about the culture and customs, and build relationships. This interaction not only enriches the migrants' experience but also facilitates mutual understanding, empathy, and social cohesion within the community.

Efforts to promote neighborhood integration should include initiatives that facilitate social interactions, encourage cultural exchanges, and celebrate diversity. By creating inclusive community spaces, organizing events, and providing platforms for dialogue, host communities can facilitate the integration process and harness the potential contributions of African migrants.

Furthermore, access to neighborhood amenities and services such as schools, healthcare facilities, public transportation, and recreational spaces is essential for African migrants to fully participate in community life. When migrants have convenient access to these services, it enhances their quality of life, allows them to actively engage in local activities, and contributes to their overall well-being.

In summary, housing and neighborhood integration are crucial for enabling African migrants to contribute fully to their new communities. By ensuring access to suitable and affordable housing, promoting diverse and inclusive neighborhoods, and providing necessary amenities and services, host communities can foster a sense of belonging, social interaction, and active participation. These factors create an environment where African migrants can thrive, contribute their skills and talents, and build a shared future with the broader community.

ACCESS TO HEALTHCARE AND SOCIAL SERVICES

Providing accessible healthcare and social services to African migrants is crucial for their well-being and integration. Ensuring equal access to healthcare, education, housing assistance, and social welfare programs helps address their specific needs and supports their integration journey.

Access to healthcare and social services is crucial for the well-being and successful integration of African migrants into their new communities. It ensures their physical and mental health, promotes social inclusion, and enables them to contribute fully to the community.

Providing healthcare services that are accessible, affordable, and culturally sensitive is essential. When African migrants have access to healthcare, they can address their health needs, receive preventive care, and manage chronic conditions. This promotes their overall well-being, allowing them to engage actively in their daily lives, including work, education, and community activities.

Moreover, access to social services such as language assistance, counseling, and settlement support plays a vital role in the integration process. These services help African migrants navigate the challenges of adapting to a new environment, providing them with the necessary information, resources, and support to meet their basic needs and achieve their goals.

Access to healthcare and social services also fosters social cohesion by promoting inclusivity and addressing disparities. When African migrants receive equitable access to these services, it sends a message of acceptance, respect, and equal rights. This fosters trust, mutual understanding, and a sense of belonging, leading to stronger community bonds.

Furthermore, access to healthcare and social services positively impacts the broader community by promoting public health and reducing healthcare disparities. When African migrants have access to necessary vaccinations, screenings, and treatments, it helps prevent the spread of diseases and promotes overall community well-being. Similarly, when social services address the needs of migrants, it contributes to community stability, safety, and social harmony.

In summary, ensuring access to healthcare and social services is crucial for African migrants to fully contribute fully to their new communities. By providing equitable access to healthcare, language assistance, settlement support, and other social services, host communities can empower migrants to address their health needs, navigate challenges, and actively engage in community life. This inclusivity creates an environment where African migrants can thrive, contribute their skills and perspectives, and

foster a shared sense of well-being and belonging with the wider community.

In conclusion, fostering integration and social cohesion for African migrants requires a comprehensive approach that addresses language acquisition, education, employment, social support, and anti-discrimination measures. When African migrants are able to fully participate in and contribute to their host societies, social cohesion is strengthened, and the benefits of diversity and cultural richness can be realized. By embracing integration as a shared responsibility, host societies can create inclusive environments where African migrants can thrive and contribute to the social, economic, and cultural fabric of their new homes.

CHAPTER 6

INTERNATIONAL COOPERATION

International cooperation regarding African migration involves collaborative efforts among nations, international organizations, and regional bodies to address the challenges and opportunities associated with migration from Africa. Such cooperation aims to ensure safe, orderly, and regular migration while protecting the rights of migrants and promoting their socioeconomic integration.

Here Are Some Key Aspects Of International Cooperation On African Migration:

REGIONAL AND CONTINENTAL FRAMEWORKS

Regional economic communities and the African Union play significant roles in fostering cooperation among African countries. For example, the African Union's Migration Policy Framework for Africa and the Regional Economic Communities' migration protocols provide guiding principles and frameworks for regional cooperation.

Firstly, regional and continental frameworks promote cooperation and coordination among participating countries. By fostering dialogue and information-sharing, these frameworks facilitate a comprehensive understanding of migration dynamics and challenges. They enable countries to work together, harmonize policies, and develop joint initiatives to address issues such as irregular migration, human trafficking, and migrant smuggling. Through enhanced coordination, countries can leverage their collective efforts to effectively manage migration flows.

Secondly, regional and continental frameworks contribute to the development of common standards and policies. By aligning migration laws and regulations, these frameworks promote consistency and coherence in migration management across participating countries. This harmonization facilitates the smooth and orderly movement of migrants, ensuring their rights and protection while respecting the sovereignty of each nation.

Furthermore, regional and continental frameworks strengthen partnerships and collaboration among countries, international organizations, and civil society. These partnerships promote the sharing of resources, expertise, and best practices, enabling stakeholders to work collectively on migration-related challenges. The pooling of resources and knowledge enhances the capacity of participating countries to address the needs of migrants and effectively respond to migration issues.

Additionally, regional and continental frameworks provide a collective voice for African countries in international forums. They amplify the concerns and interests of African nations, ensuring that their perspectives are taken into account in global migration discussions and negotiations. By speaking with a unified voice, African countries can advocate for fair and balanced migration policies, challenge negative stereotypes, and promote the rights and well-being of African migrants.

In conclusion, regional and continental frameworks have a significant impact on international cooperation for African migrants. They foster cooperation, facilitate policy harmonization, strengthen partnerships, and amplify the voices of African nations. Through these frameworks, countries can collectively address migration challenges, develop sustainable solutions, and ensure the protection and well-being of African migrants. Regional and continental cooperation remains crucial for fostering inclusive and comprehensive approaches to migration governance and maximizing the benefits of migration for all stakeholders involved.

MIGRATION DIALOG AND PARTNERSHIPS

Dialogues, consultations, and partnerships are established between African countries and destination countries or regions to address migration challenges together. These platforms facilitate information sharing, policy coordination, and joint initiatives to enhance migration management.

Migration dialogue and partnerships play a pivotal role in promoting international cooperation for African migrants. These platforms create avenues for stakeholders, including governments, international organizations, civil society, and migrants themselves, to engage in meaningful discussions, exchange knowledge, and collaborate on migration-related issues. Their impact on international cooperation is profound.

Migration dialogue and partnerships foster an environment of mutual understanding, trust, and cooperation among stakeholders. Through open and inclusive discussions, they enable the sharing of experiences, best practices, and lessons learned, leading to informed decision-making and policy development. By providing a platform for dialogue, these mechanisms facilitate the identification of common challenges and the exploration of joint solutions.

Moreover, migration dialogue and partnerships promote multilateral cooperation. They bring together countries of origin, transit, and destination, along with relevant regional and international organizations, to address migration challenges collectively. This cooperation enhances the effectiveness of efforts to combat human trafficking, smuggling, and other irregular migration practices. It also enables the pooling of resources, expertise, and technical assistance to support capacity-building initiatives in countries grappling with migration management.

Migration dialogue and partnerships have a broader impact on global migration governance. They enable African countries to influence international discussions and shape policies that are responsive to their specific contexts. By amplifying the voices of African nations, these platforms ensure that the perspectives and interests of African migrants are taken into account in global migration frameworks.

In conclusion, migration dialogue and partnerships are essential for enhancing international cooperation for African migrants. By facilitating discussions, fostering cooperation, and influencing global migration governance, these mechanisms pave the way for comprehensive and sustainable solutions to migration challenges. They promote collaboration among stakeholders, facilitate knowledge sharing, and contribute to the protection of migrants' rights and the well-being of African communities. Through effective dialogue and partnerships, the international community can work together to address the complexities of African migration and ensure the safe, orderly, and dignified movement of people across borders.

CAPACITY BUILDING AND TECHNICAL ASSISTANCE

International organizations, such as the International Organization for Migration (IOM) and the United Nations Development Programme (UNDP), support African countries in strengthening their migration governance capacities. They provide technical assistance, training, and resources to improve migration policies, data collection, border management, and migration-related services.

Capacity building programs focus on enhancing the knowledge, skills, and infrastructure necessary for effective migration governance. They provide training, workshops, and knowledge-sharing platforms to equip governments, civil society organizations, and relevant institutions with the tools needed to address migration challenges. By improving their capacity to manage migration flows, countries can better protect the rights of migrants, ensure orderly movement, and facilitate socio-economic integration. Technical assistance complements capacity building efforts by providing targeted support and expertise in areas such as data collection, policy development, and implementation. Through technical assistance, international organizations and donor countries offer guidance, resources, and advisory services to strengthen the institutional frameworks and operational capacities of countries in managing migration. This support helps countries develop evidence-based policies, establish robust migration systems, and implement effective migration-related programs.

Capacity building and technical assistance foster international cooperation by promoting knowledge exchange and collaboration among countries and stakeholders. By sharing experiences, lessons learned, and best practices, countries can learn from one another and adopt effective approaches to migration management.

Technical assistance programs also facilitate partnerships and networks, allowing for ongoing support, cooperation, and the exchange of expertise among participating countries. Moreover, capacity building and technical assistance empower African countries to engage more actively in international migration discussions and negotiations. By enhancing their knowledge and skills, countries are better equipped to participate in global forums, contribute to policy debates, and advocate for the rights and well-being of African migrants. This active engagement strengthens international cooperation, as African countries play a more significant role in shaping migration policies and frameworks.

In conclusion, capacity building and technical assistance are essential for promoting international cooperation for African migrants. By strengthening the capacity of countries and stakeholders, these initiatives enhance migration governance, facilitate knowledge sharing, and foster partnerships. They enable African nations to actively participate in global migration discussions and contribute to shaping international policies that protect the rights and welfare of migrants. Through targeted support and cooperation, capacity building and technical assistance pave the way for more effective and collaborative approaches to managing migration and harnessing its potential benefits.

MIGRATION AND DEVELOPMENT INITIATIVES

Various programs aim to leverage migration for development by promoting diaspora engagement and facilitating remittances and investments. The African Union's Initiative on Diaspora Engagement, for instance, encourages the African diaspora to contribute to the continent's development through skills transfer, knowledge sharing, and investment.

Migration and development initiatives focus on leveraging the positive aspects of migration to promote sustainable development in both countries of origin and destination. They aim to harness the skills, knowledge, and remittances of migrants to contribute to economic growth, poverty reduction, and social development. By recognizing migration as a development enabler, these initiatives foster cooperation among countries, international organizations, and stakeholders involved in migration governance. These initiatives promote dialogue, information sharing, and collaboration among countries of origin, transit, and destination. By fostering partnerships, knowledge exchange, and resource sharing, migration and development initiatives facilitate joint efforts to maximize the benefits of migration and address its challenges. They create platforms for cooperation on issues such as migrant rights, labor market integration, remittances, and diaspora engagement. Furthermore, migration and development initiatives enhance international cooperation by promoting policy coherence and coordination. They encourage countries to adopt comprehensive migration policies that align with their development objectives and consider the needs and contributions of migrants. By harmonizing policies, countries can work together to create an enabling environment for migrants to contribute fully to their host communities and support the development of their countries of origin.

Moreover, these initiatives enhance the visibility and recognition of the contributions of African migrants. They highlight the positive economic, social, and cultural impacts of migration, challenging negative narratives and stereotypes. By showcasing success stories and promoting a more balanced understanding of migration, these initiatives foster empathy, cooperation, and solidarity among countries and stakeholders.

In conclusion, migration and development initiatives are catalysts for international cooperation among African migrants. By promoting dialogue, partnerships, and policy coherence, they foster cooperation among countries and stakeholders involved in migration governance. These initiatives recognize the potential of migration to drive sustainable development and advocate for policies that leverage the contributions of migrants. Through their efforts, migration and development initiatives contribute to a more cooperative and inclusive approach to migration management, benefiting both migrants and the communities they belong to.

HUMANITARIAN AND PROTECTION MECHANISMS

International cooperation also focuses on protecting the rights and well-being of migrants, including vulnerable groups such as refugees, asylum seekers, and victims of human trafficking. Collaboration involves sharing responsibilities, supporting access to asylum procedures, providing humanitarian assistance, and combating trafficking in persons.

Humanitarian and protection mechanisms provide essential assistance and services to migrants, including access to healthcare, shelter, and legal aid. By addressing the immediate needs of migrants, these mechanisms contribute to their well-being and reduce the risks they face. International cooperation is crucial in supporting and strengthening these mechanisms, as it ensures that resources, expertise, and best practices are shared among countries, organizations, and stakeholders.

Moreover, humanitarian and protection mechanisms facilitate coordination and cooperation in managing migration flows. They foster partnerships among countries of origin, transit, and destination, along with international organizations and civil society actors. Through these partnerships, stakeholders collaborate on issues such as search and rescue operations, counter-trafficking efforts, and the provision of humanitarian aid. This cooperation enables a more comprehensive and effective response to the complex challenges posed by migration.

Furthermore, these mechanisms promote the adherence to international legal frameworks and human rights standards. They advocate for the rights of migrants, including access to asylum procedures, protection from discrimination, and the prevention of arbitrary detention. By upholding these principles, humanitarian and protection mechanisms contribute to the development of norms and practices that respect and safeguard the rights of African migrants.

In conclusion, humanitarian and protection mechanisms play a crucial role in advancing international cooperation for

African migrants. By providing essential assistance, fostering coordination, and advocating for migrants' rights, these mechanisms promote collaboration among countries, organizations, and stakeholders. International cooperation is essential in supporting and strengthening these mechanisms to ensure the protection and well-being of African migrants. Through a collective and collaborative approach, stakeholders can work together to address the humanitarian challenges faced by migrants, uphold their rights, and build a more inclusive and compassionate response to migration.

COMBATING IRREGULAR MIGRATION

Efforts are made to address the root causes of irregular migration, including poverty, conflict, environmental degradation, and lack of opportunities. This involves supporting socioeconomic development in countries of origin, promoting job creation, and addressing the drivers of migration through targeted interventions.

Firstly, combating irregular migration requires enhanced information sharing and intelligence exchange among countries and organizations. International cooperation is crucial for establishing efficient mechanisms to detect and prevent irregular migration, including the sharing of data on migration trends, routes, and smuggling networks. By working together, countries can strengthen border management, disrupt criminal networks, and improve the identification and protection of migrants in vulnerable situations.

Secondly, cooperation in combating irregular migration involves addressing the root causes that drive people to migrate irregularly. This requires collaboration on development initiatives, poverty reduction, and addressing social and economic disparities. By addressing these underlying factors, countries can create conditions that discourage irregular migration and provide alternatives for safe and regular migration pathways.

Furthermore, international cooperation is essential in providing assistance and protection to migrants affected by irregular migration. This includes cooperation in search and rescue operations, humanitarian aid provision, and ensuring access to asylum procedures for those in need of international protection. Collaborative efforts among countries and organizations are critical in ensuring the safety, well-being, and respect for the rights of African migrants throughout their migration journeys.

In conclusion, combating irregular migration requires robust international cooperation among countries and stakeholders. By sharing information, addressing root causes, and providing assistance and protection to migrants, international cooperation contributes to the effective management of migration flows and the protection of the rights of African migrants. Collaborative efforts are necessary to combat human rights abuses, disrupt smuggling networks, and provide safe and regular migration options. Through joint initiatives, countries can work together to create a comprehensive and coordinated response to irregular migration, ensuring the safety, dignity, and well-being of African migrants.

DATA AND RESEARCH

Collaboration in data collection, research, and analysis helps improve the understanding of migration trends, drivers, and impacts. Enhanced data sharing and evidence-based policymaking support effective migration management strategies.

Firstly, data and research facilitate informed decision-making and policy development. By collecting and analyzing migration data, countries and organizations can gain insights into the dynamics of migration, including its drivers, impacts, and challenges. This knowledge allows policymakers to develop evidence-based policies that address the specific needs of African migrants, promote their rights, and ensure their integration into host communities.

Secondly, data and research support the identification of gaps and areas for improvement in migration management. Through comprehensive data collection and analysis, countries and organizations can identify vulnerabilities, gaps in protection, and areas where intervention is needed. This information is instrumental in shaping collaborative efforts, resource allocation, and the development of targeted programs and services for African migrants.

Furthermore, data and research facilitate international cooperation by providing a common knowledge base for dialogue and collaboration. Shared data and research findings foster a mutual understanding of migration dynamics among countries of origin, transit, and destination. This shared understanding promotes cooperation in addressing challenges, exchanging best practices, and formulating joint strategies to enhance migration management and promote the rights of African migrants.

Additionally, data and research contribute to advocacy efforts, raising awareness about the contributions and challenges faced by African migrants. Robust research findings and data-driven narratives help dispel misconceptions and stereotypes surrounding migration.

They provide a platform for informed discussions, advocacy for migrant rights, and the development of inclusive policies that recognize and harness the potential of African migrants. **In conclusion,** data and research are essential in promoting international cooperation for African migrants. By informing decision-making, identifying gaps, fostering collaboration, and advocating for migrant rights, data and research empower countries and organizations to work together in addressing migration challenges and creating inclusive policies. Through a shared understanding of migration dynamics, stakeholders can collaborate to maximize the positive impacts of migration, protect the rights of African migrants, and promote their integration into host communities.

It's important to note that migration is a complex and multifaceted issue, and international cooperation on African migration involves numerous stakeholders working together to develop comprehensive and sustainable solutions.

CHAPTER 7

SUCCESS STORIES AND INSPIRING INDIVIDUALS

Here are a few success stories and inspiring individuals of African migrants who have had an impact on global communities

Ellen Johnson Sirleaf

Ellen Johnson Sirleaf, a Liberian politician and economist, made history as the first female president in Africa. She served as the President of Liberia from 2006 to 2018 and played a pivotal role in rebuilding the country after years of civil war. Her leadership and commitment to democracy and women's rights have been widely recognized, earning her the Nobel Peace Prize in 2011.

Ahmed Kathrada

Ahmed Kathrada, a South African anti-apartheid activist, dedicated his life to the fight against racial discrimination. He was an influential member of the African National Congress (ANC) and spent 26 years in prison, including on

Robben Island alongside Nelson Mandela. After his release, he continued to advocate for human rights and played a crucial role in South Africa's transition to democracy.

Fatou Bensouda

Fatou Bensouda, a Gambian lawyer, made history as the first African woman to serve as the Chief Prosecutor of the International Criminal Court (ICC). Her work focuses on investigating and prosecuting individuals responsible for war crimes, genocide, and crimes against humanity. Bensouda has been a strong advocate for justice and the rule of law.

Mo Farah

Mo Farah, a British long-distance runner, was born in Somalia and moved to the United Kingdom as a child. He is considered one of the greatest distance runners in modern history, winning numerous Olympic and World Championship titles. Farah's achievements have not only inspired athletes but also highlighted the potential of African migrants in sports.

Juliana Rotich

Juliana Rotich, a Kenyan technologist and social entrepreneur, co-founded Ushahidi, a platform that utilizes crowdsourcing and mapping technology for crisis response and citizen engagement. Her work has had a significant impact in areas affected by natural disasters and political unrest, empowering communities to collaborate and share information.

These success stories and inspiring individuals showcase the diverse talents, resilience, and contributions of African migrants across various fields. By sharing their stories, you can celebrate their achievements, be inspired, and highlight the valuable contributions that African migrants make to global communities.

SUMMARY

"Embracing Diversity: African Migrants' Impact on Global Communities" is a thought-provoking exploration of the experiences, contributions, and challenges faced by African migrants around the world. This book offers a comprehensive understanding of the profound impact African migrants have on the communities they join and the global landscape as a whole.

Through a collection of captivating stories and insightful analysis, this book showcases the resilience, determination, and cultural richness of African migrants. It delves into their journeys, from leaving their homelands in search of better opportunities to navigating the complexities of integration in new environments.

The book celebrates the diverse contributions of African migrants in various fields, including arts, culture, business, academia, and humanitarian work. It highlights the transformative power of intercultural exchange and how African migrants have fostered understanding, challenged stereotypes, and promoted social cohesion within their host communities.

www.ingramcontent.com/pod-product-compliance
Lightning Source LLC
Chambersburg PA
CBHW061648250726
48659CB00004B/1418